America's Eagle

Dona Herweck Rice

Publishing Credits

Rachelle Cracchiolo, M.S.Ed., *Publisher*
Conni Medina, M.A.Ed., *Managing Editor*
Jamey Acosta, *Content Director*
Dona Herweck Rice, *Series Developer*
Robin Erickson, *Multimedia Designer*

Library of Congress Cataloging-in-Publication Data

Library of Congress Control Number: 2015938708

Teacher Created Materials

5301 Oceanus Drive
Huntington Beach, CA 92649-1030
http://www.tcmpub.com

ISBN 978-1-4938-2056-6

© 2016 Teacher Created Materials, Inc.

Words to Know

eagle

egg

fly

nest